HISTORY OF FUN STUFF

The Colorful Story of COMICS

by Patricia Lakin
illustrated by Rob McClurkan

Ready-to-Read

Simon Spotlight
New York   London   Toronto   Sydney   New Delhi

Hey, kids! Some of the comics mentioned in this book are for grown-ups. Ask your parent or guardian to help you find comics appropriate for your age and reading level.

CONTENTS

Chapter 1
The Pictures Tell a Story

Imagine it's your bedtime, but instead of sleeping, you're about to read a comic book. You hide under the covers, turn on your flashlight, and flip to the first page. *Wham!* In seconds the pictures and words draw you in. You feel as if you're right in the middle of the action.

When you read comics, you feel like you're transported to another world! Did you know that, in a way, you have cavemen to thank for this?

Have you ever wondered how comic books, graphic novels, and manga came to be? Or who put the funny pages in newspapers? Did you know that history shaped superhero comics? By the time you finish reading this book, you will be a History of Fun Stuff Expert on comics. You may even want to make comics of your own!

What are comics, anyway? At their core, comics are a series of drawings arranged in a specific order to tell a story.

Each drawing in a comic is often placed inside a frame called a "panel," which is usually a square

or rectangle. In between and around the panels, spaces called "gutters" help show the passage of time from one image to the next. Speech bubbles show what characters are thinking or saying. Captions give the time or location, or comment on the story. This kind of storytelling can be traced back to cave paintings of daily life made by humans around seventeen thousand years ago!

In the ancient world, Greeks, Romans, Egyptians, and Mayans carved stories into wide slabs of stone called "friezes" (FREE-zes), which were used to decorate buildings. Mayan friezes even showed what people were saying by adding curvy lines coming from their mouths, similar to speech bubbles in modern comics!

Ancient Romans also carved a story in a spiral around a stone column called Trajan's Column.

In the eleventh century, in Japan, a priest painted picture stories on paper scrolls.

In the fourteenth century, people living in what is now Mexico painted stories in a kind of book called a codex that folds like an accordion! One codex is thirty-six feet long!

Can you imagine if you had to read comics on a building, column, or scroll? How would you share them with a friend?

For centuries, to share a written story with a friend, people had to make a copy by hand. In 1440, a German man named Johannes Gutenberg invented the printing press, and copies of books could be made easily. Without the printing press, comic books might never have been invented!

Then, in 1605, the first weekly newspaper was printed. In 1754 an editorial cartoon was published in an American newspaper for the first time. It was created by Benjamin Franklin! What are editorial cartoons? Similar to a single panel of a comic strip, editorial cartoons pair an exaggerated drawing with a caption to make people laugh, think, or both.

Franklin's cartoon showed a snake cut up into pieces, each representing a part of America, which was still a group of British colonies at that time. Below, a caption said "Join, or Die." Franklin didn't actually want anyone to die, of course. He wanted everyone to work together!

In 1837 a Swiss artist named Rodolphe Töpffer published a book for grown-ups called *The Adventures of Mr. Obadiah Oldbuck* in Switzerland. He used panels of images with captions to tell what were called "picture stories" about a man in love. Töpffer is now known as "the father of the comic strip" because his picture stories were the closest thing to comics the world had ever seen.

In 1895 the first newspaper comic was printed. Richard Outcault's *Hogan's Alley* filled up a whole page of the newspaper and told the story of a scruffy boy named for his long yellow shirt. At first, speech was written on The Yellow Kid's shirt. Then it moved to what are now called speech bubbles. The comic was an instant hit.

Comics helped sell newspapers, so the owner of another paper, William Randolph Hearst, hired Outcault and added *Hogan's Alley* to a new, special newspaper section full of comics. It was nicknamed "the Sunday funnies," or "the funny pages" section.

Readers laughed at the prankster twins in Rudolf Dirk's *The Katzenjammer Kids* and at the goofy pals in Bud Fisher's *Mutt and Jeff*.

The success led Hearst to create King Features Syndicate (SIN-duh-ket). Newspapers around the country paid the syndicate for the rights to print comics, too. Each comic was often limited to a "strip" of up to four panels arranged horizontally. The first modern-day comic strips were born!

CHAPTER 2
Comic Books to the Rescue!

In the early 1930s a man named Max Gaines printed books full of newspaper comics on cheap paper called "pulp" and sold them to large companies . . . to give away for free. Why? Giving away free books helped the companies sell their own products! The idea took off, but when the Great Depression hit, companies couldn't afford to give things away.

Gaines realized people needed entertainment and began to sell comic books at newsstands for just ten cents. They sold out! Then a man named Major

Malcolm Wheeler-Nicholson started publishing books with new comics inside, instead of comics that had already been printed in newspapers. They both hired people from around the country to dream up new comics characters. Eventually, his and Gaines's companies joined together and started a new company that would later become DC Comics.

Two longtime friends began to work at Detective Comics, one of the companies that eventually became part of DC Comics. Jerry Siegel and Joe Shuster had an idea for a comic strip about a shy boy who was secretly a superhero. Superman appeared in June 1938, just when the world needed him.

In Europe a world war was brewing, and the United States joined the fight in 1941. During World War II people craved wholesome, patriotic heroes, and comic book companies had their artists and writers create just that. There was Batman, Captain Marvel, Captain America, and Wonder Woman. Many of their outfits were red, white, and blue like the American flag. The cover of the first Captain America comic book even showed the superhero fighting the Nazi leader, Adolf Hitler. By 1943 comic books were so popular that eighteen million were sold in America each month.

Soon after World War II ended, America began competing with Russia in the Cold War. They competed to see who had the best army and most powerful weapons, and raced to put a human on the moon.

Comic book publishers created new superheroes. Many of these comics turned people's fears into strengths. Science saved the world from evil villains, while usually harmful radiation (ray-dee-AY-shun) turned normal people into superheroes.

In *The Amazing Spider-Man*, created by
Steve Ditko and Stan Lee, Peter Parker
gained his powers when he was bitten by
a radioactive spider. The comic's message,
"With great power, there must come
great responsibility," spoke to readers
and leaders alike. Lee also co-created Iron
Man, the Fantastic Four, X-Men, the Hulk,
and Thor.

Even though comics often promoted strong morals, some people thought they were too violent. In the 1950s a man named Dr. Fredric Wertham blamed comics for the country's rise in crime by young people.

In 1954 comic book publishers created the Comic Code Authority to give comics a CCA seal of approval if they followed a list of rules and were considered appropriate for kids. Many adults were still worried, so kids in that era often read comic books in secret!

CHAPTER 3
Graphic Novels, Manga, and More

The first comic books were slim booklets meant to entertain readers quickly. They focused on fictional characters and weren't seen as being very serious. Then in the 1970s, Will Eisner made a comic that told a story almost like a novel would, with drawings that were like scenes from a movie.

The panels were drawn from different angles and gave readers a feeling or mood. For example, he drew a dark room covered in shadows except for a bit of light seen through a slightly opened door, and the reader knew to be scared. He also experimented with lettering, or ways of writing the words. He used letters with jagged edges, for example, to show that a character was angry.

Eisner knew his story wasn't right for a newspaper or comic book, so he brought it to a book publisher. When asked to describe his work, a new term popped into Eisner's head. He said, "It's a graphic novel." The word "graphic" (GRAF-ick) means "related to visual arts." Eisner's book, *A Contract with God*, is considered the very first graphic novel and is for grown-up readers.

Some say the only difference between comic books and graphic novels is that comic books are held together with staples, and graphic novels are bound like many standard books. Others say graphic novels have more detailed stories, are longer, and are for older readers.

In Japan another unique form of comics was created: manga (MAHNG-gah). "Manga" is actually the Japanese word for any comic drawing. It means "whimsical" or "playful drawings." Around the world, it came to represent the style of Osamu Tezuka, who is known as the father of manga.

As a child, Tezuka loved Disney movies and Japanese comics, especially the ones influenced by *Hogan's Alley,* Outcault's newspaper comic about the boy with the long yellow shirt. As a grown-up, Tezuka

drew characters with huge eyes and spiked, colorful hair in a style of drawing that was different from anything the comic world had ever seen. One of his many popular characters, Mighty Atom, is known as Astro Boy in the United States. Tezuka even made animated films, called "anime" (AH-nee-may), in Japan.

CHAPTER 4
The Future of Comics

Just as the printing press changed everything in the fifteenth century, computers and the Internet changed how comics were read and made in the late twentieth century and beyond.

Traditionally, comics are drawn in pencil and ink. In newspapers, while the comic strips appear small on the page, they are actually drawn quite large to give artists room to add detail and write text. Then they are shrunk down to fit the size and shape of the strip in the funny pages.

With the invention of computers,

many things changed. People started
to experiment with drawing comics and
art digitally, on screen, using computer
illustration programs.

Computers became more popular.
People started reading the news online,
advertisers bought fewer newspaper
ads, and newspapers started going out of
business. Fewer newspapers meant fewer
funny pages and comic strips.

In the early twenty-first century, comic
creators realized that the Internet gave
them a new way to reach readers, even if
their comic wasn't printed in a newspaper
or comic book. They started posting
comics online as what are now called
"webcomics."

Unlike in newspaper comic strips, webcomics aren't limited to a certain number of panels. Panels can be arranged vertically (up and down), horizontally (side to side), or any way that tells a story. The panels can also be just about any size!

Even though comics are changing with the times, they aren't going away. Comic book characters are everywhere: on lunch boxes and snack food packaging, in TV shows and movies, and all over the world. Some comics have even been turned into video games!

All comics have one thing in common, whether you read them on paper or onscreen. They all use visual clues.

If one panel is larger than the rest, the action inside it is probably very important.

When your eye moves from one panel to the next, the changes in the art are clues that someone is coming closer to you or moving farther away from you, or that time is passing slowly or quickly.

The shape of a speech balloon or bubble is a clue too. A basic speech bubble "tail" points directly to the character who is speaking. A thought bubble, on the other hand, has little circles leading to the character to show that the words are what the character is thinking. Sometimes thought bubbles even look a bit like clouds. A speech bubble with a jagged or spiky tail or shape means the words inside it are coming from a TV, radio, phone, or other device, or that they are being yelled.

The size and shape of the letters inside speech bubbles and caption boxes are clues to how a character is feeling or how loudly he or she is talking. If the letters are large, the person might be shouting. If the letters are small or lowercase, or the speech bubble is made of dashed lines, the person might be whispering or scared.

There are also symbols called emanata (em-in-AH-tuh), like a lightbulb drawn above a person's head to show that he or she has an idea. It's similar to how symbols were used in ancient Egyptian hieroglyphics!

Has all this made you want to create your own comic strip or graphic novel? Well, grab a blank piece of paper or clear your computer screen and start your own chapter of comic history!

WOW!

HISTORY OF FUN STUFF

EXPERT ON

COMICS

Congratulations! You've come to the end of this book. You are now an official History of Fun Stuff Expert on comics, graphic novels, and more! Next time you see a superhero movie, you can dazzle your friends with facts about how world history played a part in inspiring the creators of the original comics! And when you pick up the funny pages or see a friend reading a graphic novel, remember all the people and inventions who, over thousands of years, made comics possible!

Hey, kids! Now that you're an expert on the history of comics, turn the page to learn even more about comics and some social studies, art, and science, too! Plus, you'll learn the basics to create your own comic!

Comics Around the World

Take a world tour of some popular comics from around the globe!:

Belgium

The Adventures of Tintin follows a young reporter who, along with his dog, takes on dangerous cases and saves the day.

France

The Adventures of Asterix follows Asterix and his friend Obélix as they travel and defend their village from Roman occupation. It has been made into many films, video games, and even a theme park!

Zig et Puce was a popular comic that started in 1925 and featured two teens who went on adventures together. It was drawn in a decorative style and was the first French comic to use speech bubbles.

Argentina

Some say the star of *Mafalda*, a comic that began in the 1960s, was like a female version of Charlie Brown from *Peanuts*.

South Africa

Nelson Mandela: The Authorized Comic Book tells the story of the leader's childhood, activism, time in prison, and election.

India

Amar Chitra Katha was created to teach children about mythology and folklore and is known for helping to launch the comic industry in India.

Nagraj, also known as the Snake King, is the star of a bestselling Indian superhero comic of the same name.

Some of these comics are meant for older readers. Head to your local comic book store to find great comics for kids.

The Tools of the Trade

While some comics are illustrated on computers, traditionally, comics are illustrated in pencil and ink. Without the graphite in pencils and the ink used in pens, comics would look very different!

After coming up with an idea, an artist called  a "penciller" sketches out the panels, characters, and action in pencil so it can be changed before moving on to the inking stage. This is because the ink used is permanent and can't be erased!

The "inker" draws over the pencil sketches with black ink using a quill pen, brush, or marker. He or she adds shading, more detail, and other finishing touches to bring the comics to life! Sometimes, after the black ink dries, color ink is added too.

Inking with India Ink

The kind of ink used to draw many comics is often called India ink or Chinese ink.

In ancient China, India, and Egypt, this ink was valued because it didn't smudge when wet and was very, very black.

It was made of fine carbon powder, which was used as a black pigment. Pigments are made of intensely colored particles that are mixed with liquid and used to give color to other materials.

In ancient times carbon powder pigment was made of carbon black or lampblack. To make carbon black, people burned wood, tar, or even animal bones until all that remained was the fine black soot, or carbon black. To make lampblack, they collected the soot from oil lamps. These materials had to be heated to just the right temperature to create pigment. The carbon powder was then pressed into sticks or cakes that could be moistened to use as ink!

Pure Pencils

You might be surprised to learn that the graphite in pencils, the pigment in India ink, and even diamonds are all made from the same element: carbon.

The carbon black used to make India ink actually changes into graphite if it is heated for a long time at five thousand four hundred degrees Fahrenheit (3,500° C). Next time you use a pencil, think about how, in a way, you're writing with a building block of diamonds!

Make Your Own Comics

Have you ever thought about making your own comic strip? There's no time like the present! Start by thinking of a story you want to tell that can be told in a few panels. For example, you could do a comic about a person with a scrawny plant. After he or she waters the plant and puts it in a sunny spot, it sprouts new leaves. When he or she talks to the plant, it grows so much that it fills the panel!

For your comic, imagine the characters and what they might say.

Next, write it all into a script with sentences that tell the story in order. Don't forget to include the characters' dialogue or speech.

Divide your story into four panels. Some of the description in your script can be included in caption boxes. Captions help tell the story by describing where the characters are or when a scene is taking place, and contain phrases like "two weeks later" or "meanwhile, at the grocery store . . ."

Now do a sketch in pencil. Feel free to erase or change things.

When you are happy with your pencil drawing, draw over the pencil lines in black ink.

Ta-da! You've made a comic strip!

Being an expert on something means you can get an awesome score on a quiz on that subject! Take this

HISTORY OF COMICS QUIZ

to see how much you've learned.

1. Which animal was the focus of Benjamin Franklin's editorial cartoon?

   a. snake
   b. elephant
   c. giraffe

2. Which war influenced the creation of Superman?

   a. Vietnam War
   b. Civil War
   c. World War II

3. Who is known as the father of the comic strip?

   a. Will Eisner
   b. William Randolph Hearst
   c. Rodolphe Töpffer

4. What does the word "manga" mean in Japanese?

   a. whimsical or playful drawing
   b. Japanese comic
   c. anime

5. Which device influenced the comics industry?

   a. printing press
   b. computer
   c. both "a" and "b"

6. Ancient people used images to tell stories on all but which one of these structures?

   a. stone column
   b. stone bridge
   c. stone friezes

7. How much did Max Gaines's comic books cost when they were first sold to the public?

   a. 10 cents
   b. 5 cents
   c. 25 cents

8. How was Will Eisner's graphic novel different from a written novel?

   a. more visual
   b. fictional
   c. shorter

9. What are comics on the Internet called?

   a. digital comics
   b. Internet comics
   c. webcomics

Answers: 1.a 2.c 3.c 4.a 5.c 6.b 7.a 8.a 9.c

HISTORY OF FUN STUFF

The Stellar Story of Space Travel

by Patricia Lakin
illustrated by Scott Burroughs

Ready-to-Read

Simon Spotlight
New York   London   Toronto   Sydney   New Delhi

CONTENTS

CHAPTER 1
The First Astronomers

Twinkle, twinkle, little star,
How I wonder what you are!

If you ever looked up at the sky and wondered, then welcome to the club. You are like millions before you. In ancient times people had no experts to ask, equipment to use, or science books to read. They looked, studied, and made guesses about outer space. Some guesses were correct, some not.

Today with a simple telescope you can see stars clearly. You might have heard that people have traveled into space *and* landed on the Moon. But do you know who the first space explorers were? And what discoveries they made? Or what science-fiction book predicted the future?

By the time you finish reading this book, you'll know the answers to all those questions and more. You will be a History of Fun Stuff Expert on space travel!

Ancient people who studied the sky were the first astronomers. Astronomy [uh-STRON-uh-mee] is the science of studying outer space. Early astronomers realized that many stars stayed in a set pattern even as they moved across the sky.

They called those patterns constellations [kon-stuh-LAY-shuns]. Early sailors and land travelers looked up at the sky and used the positions of the constellations to guide them on their way.

Ancient astronomers observed other objects in the sky that moved, like the Sun and the Moon. Huge structures were built. The shadows the buildings made on the ground or the position of the objects in the sky in relation to the structures told everyone the time and season. These buildings were the first clocks and calendars.

Stonehenge (Ancient England)

Kukulkan Pyramid (Ancient Mexico)

Temple of Amun-Ra at Karnak (Ancient Egypt)

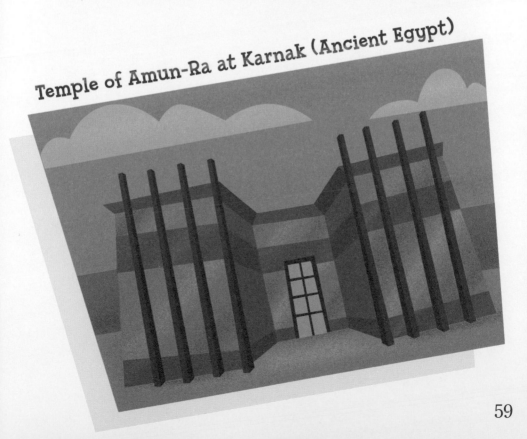

Early astronomers also noticed some objects in the sky that were different from stars, but smaller than the Sun and Moon. They called them planets. They noted that the planets moved in a circlelike path around our home planet, Earth. The famous Greek thinker Aristotle proved that Earth was shaped like a ball or sphere around 350 BC. But he believed everything circled around Earth.

More than a thousand years later the Polish astronomer Nicolaus Copernicus came to believe that the planets circled around the Sun. He knew his discovery would make people furious and scared, having their long-held beliefs questioned. He only shared some of his ideas just before he died in 1543.

The Italian Galileo Galilei was the first astronomer to take the newly invented spyglass that magnified objects and turn it into a telescope. His studies led him to agree with Copernicus. In 1632 he spoke out and was punished for his beliefs. Galileo was kept a prisoner in his home until his death in 1642.

English physicist Isaac Newton was born the year Galileo died. In 1687 Newton published his discovery—a force on Earth called gravity. It's what keeps objects on Earth from floating into space. And it's gravity that keeps planets on their path. That path, Newton discovered, is oval shaped, not round. Newton's work also proved that Copernicus and Galileo had been right—the Sun is the center of our solar system. In other words, the Earth and the other planets in our solar system orbit around the Sun.

CHAPTER 2
The Space Race Begins!

As time passed, astronomers wanted to get closer to these stars and planets. For hundreds of years people had been working on something that would eventually lead to a way to travel into space—the rocket! Around the year 1000 the Chinese created fireworks, which are really tiny rockets. Later they used them when they fought their battles by strapping fireworks onto their arrows. The lit rocket shot forward and carried the attached arrow farther and faster than ever.

After Isaac Newton's discovery, scientists knew that rockets had to fight against gravity in order to lift off the ground. The more fuel used, the farther the rocket could go.

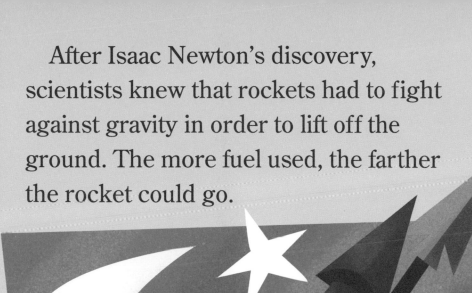

The French science-fiction writer Jules Verne dreamed of rockets and space travel. His 1865 book, *From the Earth to the Moon,* described a three-passenger rocket he named *Columbiad.* In the story the rocket was launched from Florida, flew into space, and landed on the Moon.

Actual scientists worked to make Verne's dream come true. In the early twentieth century Russian scientist Konstantin Tsiolkovsky came up with the idea of using liquid fuel to power rockets. Unlike powder, which fuels fireworks, liquid fuel can last a long time. It's still used to fuel rockets today. American scientist Robert Goddard also used liquid fuel. In 1926 his rocket made history by being the first to lift off.

On October 4, 1957, the Soviet Union, a confederation of European and Asian countries including Russia and Ukraine, launched a rocket. The rocket carried *Sputnik*, the first man-made satellite, into space. In November their second satellite was launched. This one carried a dog named Laika.

The United States was amazed at what the Soviet Union had done. The US was also working on developing rockets, but *Sputnik*'s success put the Soviet Union way ahead. *Sputnik* sparked the start of the Space Race between the Soviet Union and the United States. Ever since the end of World War II each of these powerful nations had been suspicious of the other. Who had the strongest army? Who had more advanced technology?

Soon after *Sputnik* the US president, Dwight D. Eisenhower, signed a bill that created the National Aeronautics and Space Agency, or NASA. NASA's mission: Explore outer space.

CHAPTER 3
3-2-1 Blast Off!: The Space Race Continues

January 31, 1958, was a win for the US in the Space Race. They successfully launched the satellite *Explorer 1*. But the Soviet scientists weren't resting. In April 1961 they sent the first man into space. Yuri Gagarin orbited once around Earth. The Soviet Union called their space explorers cosmonauts. The US used the term astronaut. On May 5, 1961, astronaut Alan Shepard became the first American to travel into space. Unlike Gagarin, who left his spacecraft when returning to Earth and landed by parachute, Shepard landed safely inside his space capsule.

Also unlike the Soviet mission, everything about the American mission was televised. People all over the world watched as Alan Shepard went up into space and came back.

For the next few years the United States and the Soviet Union tried to outdo the other. By 1965 Russia seemed to be in the lead when cosmonaut Alexei Leonov left his capsule and floated in space for ten minutes.

But then, that same year, US Astronaut Edward White II floated in space for twenty-three minutes! Those were great accomplishments, but landing on the moon was the big goal for both countries.

In 1969 the US accomplished something that Jules Verne had written about 104 years earlier. On July 16 the US launched a rocket from Florida. It carried three astronauts, Michael Collins, Neil Armstrong, and Buzz Aldrin. Their command module was named *Columbia*, after Verne's capsule, *Columbiad*. Four days later, Armstrong and then Aldrin left the command module, landed on the moon, and planted the American flag on its surface. It was a monumental victory.

These Americans were the first humans on the moon. But scientists knew the moon held more secrets. In 1971 and 1972 the US successfully sent up three lunar vehicles, or rovers, with astronauts to operate them. The team landed on the moon, collected rocks, and brought them back for scientists to study.

By now relations between the Soviet Union and the US had improved. In July 1975 a US and a Soviet spacecraft orbited in space at the same time. As planned, the American astronaut and the Soviet cosmonaut met in space and shook hands. The Space Race was officially over.

But space exploration was still expanding.

In 1977 Sally Ride applied to be a NASA
astronaut, and she went on to become
the first American woman in space. That
same year the space probes *Voyager 1*
and *Voyager 2* were sent into space. Their
mission: Travel to the farthest planets in
our solar system to gather and send back
information and pictures. The *Voyager*s
were built to last for five years.

Sadly, not all of NASA's missions in space were successful. On a cold Florida morning in January 1986 the spacecraft *Challenger* launched. It carried a crew of seven. A little more than a minute after liftoff the rocket carrying *Challenger* exploded. All aboard were killed. Later, scientists discovered that a sealing ring in the fuel tank had broken, which may have caused the explosion. The world was saddened.

CHAPTER 4:
Space Exploration Today and Tomorrow

Space exploration had to go on. Sending people into space wasn't the only way to do it. And some planets are so far away that no person could make the trip—at least not currently. Mars is the closest planet to Earth and is about 140 million miles away! Mechanical robots, used during the Space Race, were the answer. But scientists didn't want the robots to crash or get damaged upon landing. In the late 1990s they came up with a clever solution for the *Mars Pathfinder*. Once it reached

Mars, parachutes opened and lowered it down. Then airbags popped up so that it bounced safely on the surface of Mars. *Mars Pathfinder* analyzed samples of rock and dirt and transmitted its findings back to Earth for scientists to study.

Since the 1960s, the US and other countries have sent unmanned satellites up to orbit the Earth. Some are weather satellites. They send back images of Earth that show clear skies, patches of clouds, or storms that are forming. That information helps us prepare for upcoming weather. Communication satellites either receive signals from Earth or bounce them back to Earth. They're used when we make some phone calls or tune in to some radio stations or watch some television channels.

Scientists also rely on other unmanned
satellites called space probes. *Voyager 1*
and *Voyager 2* are the space probes that
were only supposed to last until 1982.
They are *still* hurtling far off into space. In
2012 *Voyager 1* entered the space beyond
the planets in our solar system, called
interstellar space. *Voyager 1* has now
traveled farther than anyone or anything
from Earth has ever traveled before.

Today scientists from all over the world realize that information we gather from outer space needs to be shared. In the late 1990s many countries worked together to launch the International Space Station, or ISS.

Since 2000, men and women from a variety of countries have taken turns living on board the ISS. It is a huge orbiting beehive of scientific activity. Astronauts, scientists, and other experts conduct experiments there. It gives them the

chance to do research with no pull of gravity.

One of the things these experts are studying is how the human body is affected in space with no gravity. Bones and muscles weaken. How can people keep their bodies strong? This research will lead to solutions for people who will travel and one day may live in space.

Today you don't have to be an astronaut to go into orbit. In the early 2000s a few millionaires who passed a physical test went aboard the International Space Station. One person paid $35 million for his ticket. Another got a bargain and paid $20 million! More and more, scientists in many countries realize that space travel

needs to be open to other citizens. One businessperson has created a spacecraft and is selling tickets for $250,000 each. The hope is that traveling into outer space will become cheaper and more common. Who knows? If you are in shape, in a few years you may be planning your vacation—in outer space.

SPACE RESORT

HISTORY
OF FUN STUFF
EXPERT
ON
SPACE
TRAVEL

Congratulations! You've come to the end of this book. You're now an official History of Fun Stuff Expert on space travel. Go ahead and impress your friends and family with all the cool things you know about space. And the next time you gaze up at the sky, remember everything you've learned and ask yourself: Do you want to go up to space someday?

Hey, kids! Now that you're an expert on the history of space travel, turn the page to learn even more about space travel and some astronomy, world cultures, and literature along the way!

Day and Night

You probably know that the Earth orbits around the Sun, and that it takes the Earth one year to complete one full orbit. But did you know that the Earth spins as it orbits?

Just like a ballet dancer spins on his or her toes, the Earth spins on its axis. The Earth's axis is an imaginary line that runs through the planet from the North Pole to the South Pole. The Earth rotates around this imaginary line.

You see, even though the Sun appears to travel across the sky, rising in the east in the morning and setting in the west at night, the Sun isn't actually moving at all—we are!

It takes the Earth twenty-four hours to complete one full spin on its axis. At any given moment it's daytime for the half of the Earth that is being lit by the Sun. But at the same time the side of the Earth that is facing away from the Sun is experiencing nighttime.

If you have a globe and a flashlight at home, you can try this yourself! Shine a flashlight on the globe and have a friend spin the globe around slowly. Notice how the side facing the flashlight is always bright, while the side opposite the flashlight is always dark, just like the day and night!

The Stars that Shaped the Sky

In ancient times people looked at the stars and saw pictures. Each picture, called a constellation, had its own story. These stories were told by people all over the world!

Orion, the Hunter—There are many stories about the Orion constellation. The ancient Greeks said Orion was a great hunter who fell in love with Artemis, the goddess of the hunt. But the ancient Egyptians associated this constellation with their god of rebirth, Osiris. This constellation is very big and very bright. In North America you can find Orion easily any time from November through February.

The Big Dipper—Believe it or not, the Big Dipper actually isn't a constellation; it's an asterism! An **asterism** is a group of stars that form part of a constellation. The Big Dipper is part of the constellation Ursa Major, or the Great Bear. Many cultures have stories about the Big Dipper. In Germany and Hungary the asterism is known as a cart or wagon, and in the United Kingdom and Ireland people see it as a plow. To find the Big Dipper from the continental United States, look to the northwest sky in the summer.

Cygnus, the Swan—Some ancient Greeks saw this constellation as Zeus, the god, disguised as a swan, but other Greeks said the swan was Orpheus, a musician who transformed into a swan after his death. The ancient Chinese also had a myth about this constellation—they saw the constellation as a bridge across the heavens. Two forbidden lovers would meet once a year by crossing the starry bridge. If you live in the continental United States, you can find Cygnus by looking for the Northern Cross, an asterism within the constellation. You can find it high in the sky during late summer.

Leo, the Lion—Leo is one of the oldest documented constellations. The ancient Greeks saw Leo as the lion that the hero Hercules killed during his twelve labors, and this same constellation was also seen as a lion by the ancient Egyptians, Sumerians, Persians, and Babylonians. In North America you can find Leo during the springtime by looking for his mane, a backward question mark.

Science Fiction That Came True!

In 1865 Jules Verne wrote about astronauts landing on the moon. No one believed it would happen—but a little more than one hundred years later, it did!

Verne wrote **science fiction**. Science fiction is a genre about imaginary scientific developments.

Verne wasn't the only writer or artist to predict something. In the late 1400s Leonardo da Vinci, the Italian artist who painted the *Mona Lisa*, drew sketches of a flying machine. He hoped that one day humans could fly in machines—and he was right.

Mark Twain, the author of *The Adventures of Huckleberry Finn*, wrote about something that resembles today's Internet back in 1898. But it wasn't just the Internet—Twain predicted social media, too! He wrote that one day we'd be able to make our thoughts public with the click of a button. Little did he know, today this system also helps space explorers communicate with people back on Earth.

In the TV show, *Star Trek: The Next Generation*, which premiered in 1987, members of the starship *Enterprise* used PADDs, or "personal access display devices." PADDs sent messages and recorded data. Now we use tablets for the same purpose.

In the late 1970s author Douglas Adams penned *The Hitchhiker's Guide to the Galaxy*. He wrote about a machine that can make any drink instantly! Today NASA is developing a 3-D food printer. The printer will make food for astronauts on long space flights. It can print a tasty pizza, made with special "ink" for the bread, sauce, and cheese.

What else are today's scientists working on? What about warp speed? Although it seems impossible now, maybe someday we will be able to launch spaceships farther into space. You can see spaceships travel at warp-speed in science-fiction movies and television shows like *Star Wars* and *Star Trek*.

What do you think life will be like in one hundred or one thousand years? Maybe we'll vacation on Saturn—or fly our very own spaceships!

Being an expert on something means you can get an
awesome score on a quiz on that subject! Take this

HISTORY OF SPACE TRAVEL QUIZ
to see how much you've learned.

1. Early sailors and travelers used star patterns called what to guide them?
   a. constellations   b. black holes   c. telegrams

2. Which astronomer was the first to believe that the planets circled around the Sun?
   a. Aristotle   b. Sally Ride   c. Nicolaus Copernicus

3. What force, discovered by Newton, keeps objects on Earth from floating into space?
   a. potatoes   b. gravity   c. magnification

4. Where were rockets invented around the year 1000?
   a. China   b. the Moon   c. England

5. When did the Soviet Union launch *Sputnik*, the first man-made satellite, into space?
   a. 1957   b. 1090   c. 1832

6. Which US president signed the bill that created NASA?
   a. Teddy Roosevelt   b. James Garfield   c. Dwight D. Eisenhower

7. Unlike the first cosmonaut in space, the first American astronaut in space was
   able to do what?
   a. the hokey pokey   b. talk to extraterrestrials   c. land safely back on Earth
                                                              inside his space capsule

8. What year did US astronauts land on the Moon for the first time?
   a. 1320   b. 1969   c. 1997

9. In the 1990s what robot did scientists send to Mars?
   a. *Mars Pathfinder*   b. *Mars Enterprise*   c. *Mars Penguin*

10. What part of space did the space probe *Voyager 1* enter in 2012?
    a. the Sun   b. groovy space   c. interstellar space

Answers: 1. a 2. c 3. b 4. a 5. a 6. c 7. c 8. b 9. a 10. c

96

HISTORY OF FUN STUFF

The Scoop on Ice Cream!

by Bonnie Williams
illustrated by Scott Burroughs

Ready-to-Read

Simon Spotlight
New York   London   Toronto   Sydney   New Delhi

CONTENTS

CHAPTER 1
The Origins of Ice Cream

You know lots of things about ice cream, right? You know it's delicious, and you know your favorite flavor. You also know that ice cream comes in cups or cones and that you eat it with a spoon or just lick it right off the scoop. But what do you know about the history of ice cream? Do you know who invented it and when? Or which United States presidents loved ice cream?

Today if you have a hankering for ice cream, it is easy enough to find some—you just buy it from the supermarket or go to your favorite ice-cream parlor and order a scoop (or two!).

But did you know it wasn't always so easy to satisfy your craving? And do you know where those scoops came from or how they were made? That's where this book comes in. By the time you finish reading this book, you will know the answers to these questions and many more. You will be a History of Fun Stuff Expert on ice cream!

The history of ice cream is not an easy one to piece together. Sometimes it seems about as clear as a bowl of ice-cream soup, and just as messy! What historians do know for surc is that frozen treats have been enjoyed for at least two thousand years.

In ancient times, snow and ice were combined with flavors like honey, fruit, and juice. Nero, a Roman emperor who ruled ancient Italy from the year 54 to the year 68, would make his slaves run up high into the mountains for ice.

When the slaves returned, they added fruit and juice to the ice to make something we'd recognize today as a slushie or Italian ice.

The Chinese were probably the first to mix ice and snow with milk, making a creamy dish that more closely resembles the ice cream we know and love today. There is a record of frozen dairy treats made of milk, flour, and camphor as far back as the Tang Dynasty that began in the year 618 and ended in 907. Camphor is a substance that comes from the camphor tree. It has a very strong smell. Today camphor is used in mothballs, gels to help with colds, and insect repellent. Just don't eat any of those!

CAMPHOR TREE
ICE CREAM

It took centuries for ice cream to make its way from China to Europe. There are many legends about how it did so. One of the most famous ones involves a man you may have already heard of named Marco Polo. In the 1200s, he traveled from Italy to China. Some say that he returned with recipes for ice cream, but there is no

evidence to support this. Regardless, by the 1600s, ice cream was enjoyed throughout Europe, and in the later half of the century, it was being served at the royal court of England. Not long after this, ice cream arrived in the American colonies.

CHAPTER 2
Almost Modern History

Ice cream has been a part of the American way of life since the very beginning, even before the Declaration of Independence was signed in 1776. When the states were still colonies of England, the well-to-do would serve ice cream at parties and other events.

One night in 1744, the governor of the Maryland colony served ice cream after dinner. We know about this because one of his guests was so amazed by the dessert that he wrote about it in a letter. This is the oldest record of ice cream in the Americas.

Our founding fathers and mothers had a real sweet tooth for ice cream too. In 1790, George Washington was a year into being the first president of the United States. That summer, he and his wife, Martha, spent $200 on ice cream. That's a lot of money, but it's even more when you think about how much that would be worth today.

Unfortunately, it's hard to calculate the value of money from that far back, but we do know that as little as one hundred years ago, $200 was worth more than $4,700! How much ice cream do you think you could buy with that much money?

Another founding father and the third president of the United States, Thomas Jefferson, is known for having done many things. He wrote the Declaration of Independence and started his own university, the University of Virginia. But did you know that he also loved ice cream? He kept a recipe for vanilla ice cream written in his own handwriting.

He discovered this recipe in France, where he was an ambassador before he became the American president. When he returned to the United States, he would often serve ice cream at his parties. If you had been seated at Thomas Jefferson's table, there is a good chance you would have eaten ice cream based on this recipe.

ICE-CREAM
RECIPE

Until the mid-1800s, making ice cream was hard work that took hours to be done by hand. Then, in 1843, a woman named Nancy Johnson patented the first ice-cream maker that made the work a bit easier. Here's how her machine worked:

You'd start with two cans, one smaller, one larger. In the smaller can, you would add your basic ice-cream ingredients like milk, sugar, and flavoring. Then you would add ice and salt to the larger can and fit the smaller can inside.

Next you'd use a crank to churn the ingredients in the smaller can. This made the mixture smooth and creamy, while the ice in the larger can simultaneously froze it.

After about twenty to forty-five minutes of cranking, you could enjoy your ice cream.

Sound like fun? If you want to make ice cream the old-fashioned way, there are companies that still sell ice-cream makers based on Nancy Johnson's original design.

Because of Nancy Johnson's invention, more people were able to experience the joy of eating ice cream. Another turning point came a few years later, in 1851, when a man named Jacob Fussell opened the first ice-cream factory. As you might expect, his business boomed, and he soon opened up other factories. For the first time in its long history, ice cream was being manufactured on a large scale. To this day, Jacob Fussell is known as the father of the ice-cream industry.

FATHER OF THE ICE-CREAM INDUSTRY

JACOB FUSSELL

CHAPTER 3
The Scoop on Scoops—
Cones, Sundaes, and More!

With ice cream available to everyone, the stage was now set for classic ice-cream dishes to take shape. And speaking of taking shape, you might not believe it, but there was a time when the ice-cream cone didn't exist. It's hard to pinpoint exactly who invented the cone.

The best evidence shows that there were a number of people who independently came up with the idea of eating ice cream out of edible cones. However, cones weren't popular until the St. Louis World's Fair in 1904 where many vendors sold them. After that, there was no turning back. The ice-cream cone was here to stay!

What about ice-cream sundaes? Like the invention of the ice-cream cone, the origin of the ice-cream sundae is up for debate. Some believe that it was invented in 1881 in Two Rivers, Wisconsin, when chocolate sauce was drizzled on top of scoops of ice cream.

Others say it was 1892, in Ithaca, New York, when cherry syrup and a cherry were added to a dish of ice cream. In both stories, the dish was named after the day, Sunday, on which it was either invented or often served. Today there's a friendly rivalry between Ithaca and Two Rivers about the true birthplace of the sundae.

Last but not least, what about ice-cream novelties? No frozen section of a grocery store would be complete without ice-cream sandwiches, pops, and bars. How and when did they come about? The first ice-cream novelty was vanilla ice cream covered in a chocolate shell, known as an Eskimo Pie.

It was invented in 1920 by a high school teacher in Iowa who also sold ice cream. He got inspired by an eight-year-old customer who couldn't decide between buying a chocolate bar or ice cream. Since both are delicious, the teacher came up with a way of combining them!

CHAPTER 4
Ice Cream Today

As you know, you can find ice cream everywhere these days. It is so much a part of our culture that when immigrants arrived on Ellis Island in the early 1900s, they were served ice cream. Today almost ten percent of milk production in the United States goes into the manufacturing of ice cream in every flavor and type imaginable. The ice-cream industry makes a profit of ten billion dollars every year!

How does the ice-cream industry make so much money? It's because Americans love ice cream! The average American eats about eighty cups of ice cream every year. Depending on the size of your scoop, that's two to four scoops every four and a half days!

Ice cream has been so popular that in 1984, Ronald Reagan, the fortieth president of the United States, named July as National Ice-Cream Month. Every year, the official National Ice-Cream Day is the third Sunday of July.

Do you know what the most popular flavor of ice cream is in the United States?

The answer probably won't surprise you. It's vanilla, followed by chocolate. Combined, they make up about fifty percent of ice-cream sales. Which of those two flavors do you prefer? Do you have another favorite flavor? Do you know which flavor is your best friend's favorite?

As you can probably imagine, ice cream isn't just popular in the United States. People in other countries love ice cream too. But what are some favorite flavors around the world? In Japan, there's an ice-cream flavor made with squid ink.

GARLIC ICE CREAM

FISH EGG ICE CREAM

SQUID INK ICE CREAM

And you can find ice cream topped with caviar, also known as fish eggs, in France. But not to be outdone, the United States also makes its share of unique flavors. You can find pizza-flavored ice cream, bacon-flavored ice cream, and even garlic-flavored ice cream! Would you eat any of these flavors? Can you think of other flavors you've never heard of but would be willing to try?

EXPERT

HISTORY
OF FUN STUFF
EXPERT
ON
ICE
CREAM

Congratulations! You've come to the end of this book. You are now an official History of Fun Stuff Expert on ice cream. Go ahead and impress your friends and family with all the cool things you know about the world's coolest treat. And the next time you take a lick off your scoop of ice cream, think about the years of history that went into it and enjoy!

Hey, kids! Now that you're an expert on the history of ice cream, turn the page to learn even more about it and some geography and science along the way!

Ice Cream Around the World

Check out these fascinating flavors we found from different countries all over the world. Which ones sound good to you?

Argentina: *Dulce de leche* Ice Cream — A smooth and tasty dessert that is popular in South America, "*dulce de leche*" means "caramel" in Spanish, and it makes this flavor of ice cream extra sweet.

France: Caviar Ice Cream — In France you can try caviar-flavored ice cream, made with real caviar (otherwise known as fish eggs!).

Germany: Apple Strudel Ice Cream — "Strudel" is a flaky pastry with a creamy flavored filling that is a traditional dessert in Germany. This flavor of ice cream tastes just like it.

Israel: Cardamom Ice Cream — A common ingredient in Middle Eastern recipes, cardamom is a strong spice that gives this ice-cream flavor a kick!

Japan: Squid Ink Ice Cream — A squid is a marine animal similar to an octopus that has a long head and two extra-long tentacles. Squid ink is used in many pasta dishes throughout Asia, but if you travel to Japan you can also try squid ink–flavored ice cream. We hear it tastes salty!

New Zealand: Hokey Pokey Ice Cream — In New Zealand, "Hokey Pokey" ice cream consists of vanilla ice cream with pieces of crunchy honeycomb toffee inside.

Philippines: Cheese Ice Cream — In the Philippines, you'll find chunks of actual cheddar cheese in this savory-sweet ice cream.

Singapore: Chili Pepper Ice Cream — This spicy ice-cream flavor comes from Singapore, where hot chili peppers are blended with a tomato-based ice cream.

Hope you enjoyed this sweet trip around the world! If you could invent your own flavor of ice cream, what would it be?

The Science of Making Ice Cream

Today ice cream is usually made with the big industrial machines used in factories, or the simple countertop ice-cream makers used at home. But as you learned, Nancy Johnson started it all in 1843, when she invented a hand-cranked machine that could churn out ice cream faster than ever before!

Johnson's hand-cranked ice-cream maker used a simple **endothermic reaction** to freeze ice cream. But what is an endothermic reaction?

A **reaction** happens when one thing becomes another. For example, when you leave a can of soda open for too long, it will lose its fizz. This happens because the carbon dioxide (the fizzy bubbles) in soda changes from a liquid to a gas, rises to the top of the soda, and then escapes into the air.

The word **endothermic** is used to describe any process that requires heat. Using heat to melt ice cubes into water is an endothermic process.

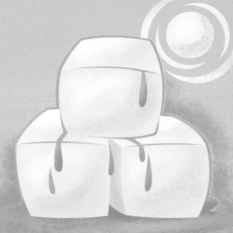

So, an **endothermic reaction** is a reaction that requires heat to turn one thing into another. Baking a cake is a great example of an endothermic reaction: A set of ingredients, like flour, sugar, and eggs, plus heat from the oven, react to create a cake.

Now that we know what an endothermic reaction is, let's take a look at a hand-cranked ice-cream maker. These ice-cream makers have three parts: an **outer bucket**, an **inner container**, and a **mixing tool**.

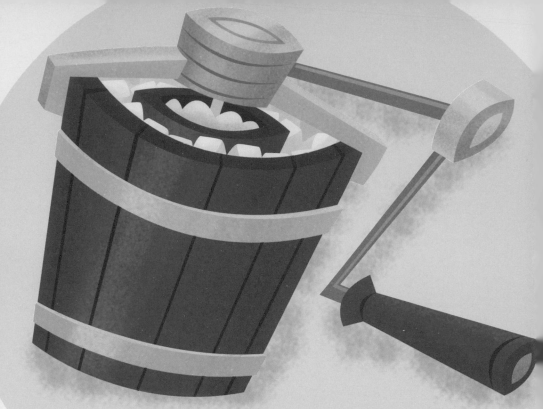

To make ice cream, you pour the ingredients into the inner container, which is then sealed shut with the mixing tool inside. Next you fill the outer bucket with ice and salt, fitting the inner container in the middle of the ice-salt mixture.

When salt mixes with ice, it causes an **endothermic reaction**. The reaction sucks up all of the heat from its surroundings, freezing the ice cream inside the inner container. The salt also lowers the freezing point of the ice, allowing the ice-salt mixture to get as cold as -21° Celsius. That is really cold!

While the **endothermic reaction** takes place, the mixing tool stirs the ice cream inside. As the ice cream is stirred, the liquid ingredients freeze into a creamy solid.

Who knew science could be so delicious?

Fun Fact! Do you know why we pour salt on snowy sidewalks? As we've just seen in our ice-cream maker, salt lowers the freezing point of water. This means that salt both melts the snow on walkways *and* makes it much harder for the water to refreeze unless it gets very, very cold. Presto! No more slippery sidewalks in the winter!

Being an expert on something means you can get an
awesome score on a quiz on that subject! Take this

HISTORY OF ICE CREAM QUIZ

to see how much you've learned.

1. Frozen treats have been enjoyed for at least _____ years.

a. 100   b. 450,000   c. 2,000

2. Which emperor ruled the Roman Empire from the year 54 to the year 68 AD?

a. Alexander   b. Nero   c. Augustus

3. The first president of the United States, _____, spent $200 on ice cream in just one summer!

a. George Washington   b. Zachary Taylor   c. Abraham Lincoln

4. Thomas Jefferson discovered a recipe for ice cream while serving as ambassador to which country?

a. Russia   b. France   c. Holland

5. Ice cream wasn't made in factories until what year?

a. 1492   b. 1957   c. 1851

6. The ice-cream cone became popular at the world's fair in _____.

a. Shanghai   b. Alexandria   c. St. Louis

7. When immigrants arrived at _____ in the early 1900s, they were served ice cream.

a. Ellis Island   b. San Francisco   c. Chicago

8. What do Argentina's *dulce de leche* ice cream and Germany's apple strudel ice cream have in common?

a. Both contain squid ink.   b. Both are based on popular desserts.
c. Nothing! They are completely different.

Answers: 1. c 2. b 3. a 4. b 5. c 6. c 7. a 8. b